THE POWER OF MANTRA

UNDERSTANDING THE SCIENCE AND PRACTICE OF INDIAN CHANTING

DR. JAGADEESH PILLAI

Made with ♥ on the Notion Press Platform
www.notionpress.com

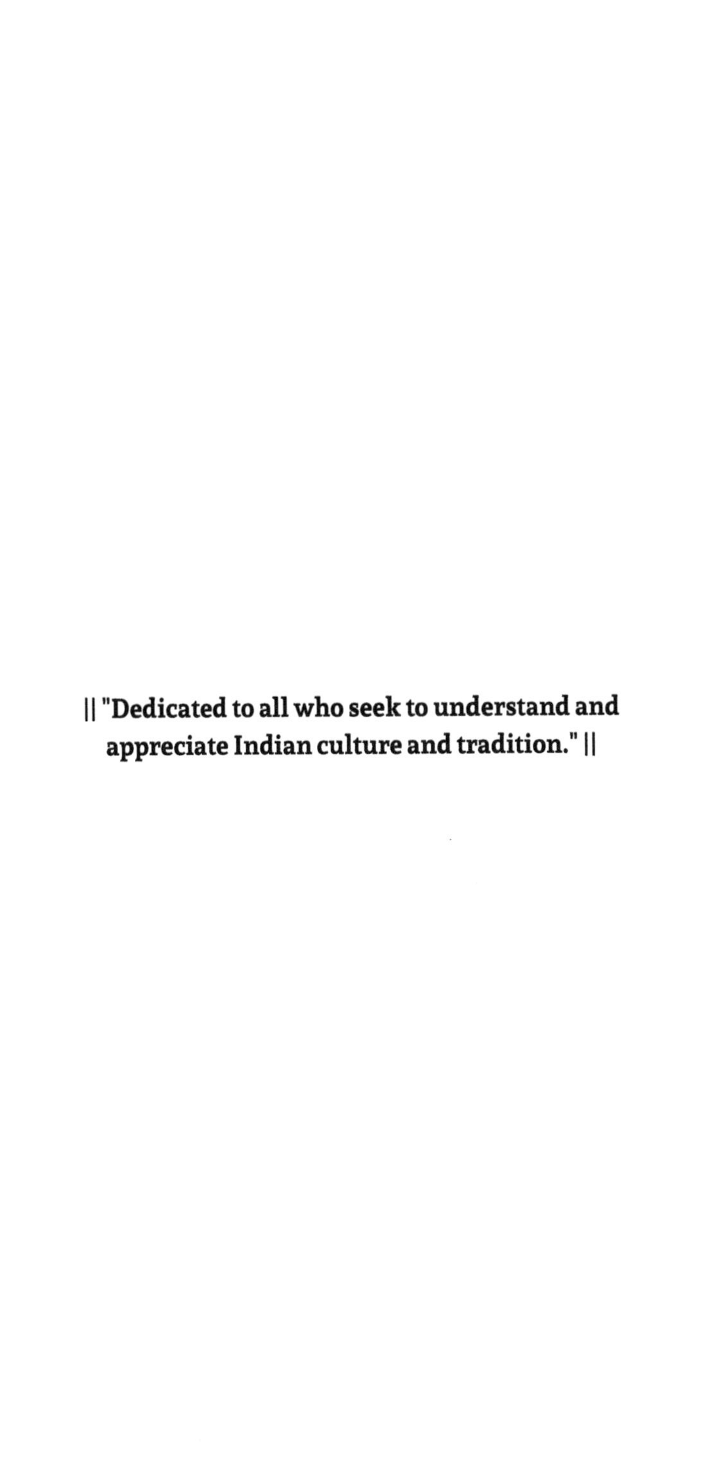

|| "Dedicated to all who seek to understand and appreciate Indian culture and tradition." ||

Contents

Contents

Prayer

"Om Gam Ganapataye Namaha"
- "Salutations to the elephant-faced deity"

About The Author

Dr. Jagadeesh Pillai is a renowned Guinness World Record holder, writer, and researcher hailing from Varanasi, also known as the abode of Lord Shiva. With a Ph.D. in Vedic Science and a range of creative ideas and achievements, he is a true polymath. He is the author of more than 100 books including Research Publications. Although his roots can be traced back to Kerala, the people of Varanasi hold him in high regard and affectionately consider him one of their own.

Dr. Pillai has achieved four Guinness World Records in the following subjects:

"Script to Screen" - In this record, Dr. Pillai produced and directed an animation film within the shortest time possible, breaking the previous record set by Canadians. He has also received numerous national and international awards and recognitions for this achievement.

Longest Line of Postcards - For this record, Dr. Pillai created a line of 16,300 postcards on the occasion of the 163rd anniversary of Indian Postal Day. The event also included a questionnaire about the Indian flag.

Largest Poster Awareness Campaign - Dr. Pillai designed an awareness campaign on the subject of "Beti Bachao - Beti Padhao" (Save the Girl Child - Educate the Girl Child) to achieve this record.

Largest Envelope - In tribute to the Indian Prime Minister's

"Make in India" initiative, Dr. Pillai created a 4000 square meter envelope using waste paper to achieve this record.

Attempted - **70000 Candles on a 210 kg Cake** - To celebrate the 70th Indian Independence Day, Dr. Pillai attempted to light 70,000 candles on a 210 kg cake, which was recorded in World Records India.

Attempted - **Documentary on Dhamek Stupa of Sarnath in 17 Languages** - Dr. Pillai attempted to create a documentary on the Dhamek Stupa of Sarnath, dubbing it in 17 different languages. The result of this attempt is currently awaiting confirmation from the Guinness World Records.

Dr. Pillai is skilled in teaching the Bhagavad Gita, a Hindu scripture, and is popular among young people. He has helped many young people improve their lives through his motivational teachings.

In addition to teaching, he has composed and sung numerous Sanskrit Bhajans and patriotic songs.

He has also written and directed several short films and documentaries for awareness campaigns, and has volunteered with the police in both UP and Kerala to spread awareness about various issues through videos and photography.

Incredibly, he has produced and directed over 100 documentaries about the city of Varanasi, all on his own.

He has also helped and guided more than 25 boys and girls to achieve world records through creative and innovative methods. He is a multifaceted person who uses his intellect and the blessings given to him by God to excel in various areas. He is both a teacher and a student, always learning and teaching, and is able to master any subject he comes across.

He is a selfless social activist and motivational speaker who has overcome struggles and failures to become a successful and enthusiastic individual with a rich life experience.

In addition to his work with the Bhagavad Gita, he is also an efficient Tarot card reader, Astro-Vastu consultant, and a talented singer and composer. He has sung the entire Ram Charita Manas and Bhagavad Gita in his own compositions, and has sung the phrase "Lokah Samastha Sukhino Bhavantu" in 50 different languages. He is currently working on a detailed and scientific study of Vedas, Upanishads, Puranas, and the Bhagavad Gita. He has also composed and sung the Hanuman Chalisa and Gayatri Mantra in 108 and 1008 different compositions, respectively.

Awards - Four Times Guinness World Records, Winner of Mahatma Gandhi Vishwa Shanti Puraskar, Mahatma Gandhi Global Peace Ambassador, Kashi Ratna Award, Dr. APJ Abdul Kalam Motivational Person of the Year 2017, Mother Teresa Award, Indira Gandhi Priyadarshini Award, Bharat Vikas Ratna Award, Udyog Ratna Award, Vigyan Prasar Award, Poorvanchal Ratn Samman.

Preface

The Power of Mantra: Understanding the Science and Practice of Indian Chanting is a comprehensive guide to the ancient tradition of Indian chanting and its spiritual and therapeutic benefits. This book delves into the science and practice of Indian chanting, examining the role of mantra in Hinduism and Indian spirituality, the phonetics and meaning of mantra, and how sounds affect the mind and body.

The book also covers the role of raga and tala in Indian chanting, the importance of pronunciation and intention, the different types of mantra, and the history and development of Indian chanting and mantra traditions. Additionally, it explores the power of Nada Yoga in Indian chanting, the role of the guru, and the use of mantra in Ayurveda and Indian healing traditions.

Furthermore, this book will also discuss the relationship between mantra and the chakras, the use of mantra in yoga, meditation, and daily life, the role of mantra in devotional practice and Bhakti Yoga, and the effect of group chanting and community practice.

This book is intended for anyone interested in learning more about the rich tradition of Indian chanting and the powerful effects of mantra on the mind, body, and spirit. Whether you are a beginner or an experienced practitioner, this book will provide you with a deeper understanding of the science and practice of Indian chanting.

I

Science and Practice of Mantra Chanting

Mantra chanting is an ancient practice that has been used for thousands of years in India to achieve spiritual growth, emotional balance, and physical well-being. The power of mantra lies in its ability to tap into the universal energy and consciousness, leading to a deep sense of inner peace and connection with the divine.

In this book, we will explore the science and practice of Indian chanting, including the history and origins of mantra, the different types of mantras and their meanings, and the various techniques for practicing mantra chanting. We will also delve into the benefits of mantra chanting and how it can be used to improve physical and mental health, as well as to achieve spiritual growth and enlightenment.

The practice of mantra chanting has its roots in the Vedic tradition of India, dating back to over 5,000 years ago. Mantra chanting was traditionally passed down from teacher to student, and was used for a variety of purposes, including healing, meditation, and spiritual growth.

There are many different types of mantras, each with its own unique meaning and purpose. Some mantras are used for specific purposes, such as healing or protection, while others are used for general well-being and spiritual growth. Some of the most common types of mantras include the Om or Aum mantra, the Gayatri Mantra, and the Maha Mrityunjaya Mantra.

Mantra chanting can be done alone or in a group, and can be practiced in a variety of settings, including at home, in a temple or ashram, or even in nature. The most important aspect of mantra chanting is the intention and focus behind the practice.

The benefits of mantra chanting are many and varied, including improved physical and mental health, increased emotional balance and inner peace, and spiritual growth and enlightenment. In this book, we will explore the scientific and spiritual aspects of mantra chanting, and provide guidance for incorporating this powerful practice into your daily life.

Surely, the science and practice of Indian chanting is a powerful tool for achieving spiritual growth, emotional balance, and physical well-being. Through this book, you will gain a deeper understanding of the history, meaning, and techniques of mantra chanting, as well as the benefits it can bring to your life.

"**Om**"

- represents the universe and everything in it

II

The Role of Mantra in Hinduism and Indian Spirituality

Mantra is a central part of Indian spirituality and Hinduism. It combines the power of words, sounds, and vibrations. Used for thousands of years, mantras explore the divine that resides within us and create powerful spiritual connections.

Mantras evoke the power of the divine through mantra sound. In Sanskrit, the language of ancient India, mantra literally means "that which protects the mind" — and it practices are spiritual protectors. Specific mantras create the sacred environment necessary to bring peace and healing. By chanting a mantra one is inviting a frequency of divine energy that promotes mental clarity and peace of heart.

Mantras not only create an opening to the spiritual world; they also become a gateway to knowledge and meditation. Chanting a mantra is a direct route to experiencing personal transformation and divine connection. The energy and vibration that is created by mantras helps to open and awaken the spiritual power within us as well as to channel it in a healthy, balanced, and harmonious way. Mantras are an anchor for positive thought, an invitation to become still and connect with the divine.

The power of mantras comes not only from the sound and meaning but also from the spiritual vibration generated from their repetition. There is an element of sacredness in mantras that bring people closer to their spirituality, making them ultimately feel connected and empowered. The process of repeating mantras is a skill that develops over time, and with repeated practice, it is a powerful tool for healing, insight and relaxation.

Mantras offer an exciting way to explore spirituality and experience greater peace and connection with the divine. They have an extremely powerful and profound impact, allowing us to reduce stress, increase clarity, and become more aware of our surroundings. A daily practice of repeating mantras is an incredibly powerful tool to help one become more mindful and develop a deeper connection with the divine.

"Om Namah Shivaya"

- "I honor the divinity within me"

III

How Sounds Affect the Mind and Body

The Phonetics and Meaning of Mantra: How Sounds Affect the Mind and Body.

In the previous chapter, we introduced the concept of mantra chanting and its origins in the Vedic tradition of India. In this chapter, we will delve deeper into the phonetics and meaning of mantras, and explore how the sounds and vibrations of mantras can affect the mind and body.

Mantras are usually made up of a combination of syllables, words, or phrases in Sanskrit, which is considered to be the most sacred language in India. The sounds and vibrations of Sanskrit are believed to have a powerful effect on the mind and body, and can be used to tap into the universal energy and consciousness.

The phonetics of mantras play a crucial role in their effectiveness. The sounds of the mantras are believed to create specific vibrations in the body, which can have a positive impact on physical and mental health. For example, the Om or Aum mantra is believed to vibrate at the same frequency as the universe, and can be used to achieve a state of deep relaxation and inner peace.

The meaning of mantras also plays an important role in their effectiveness. Each mantra is believed to have a specific meaning and purpose, and can be used for a variety of purposes, such as healing, protection, and spiritual growth. For example, the Gayatri Mantra is a powerful mantra for spiritual growth and enlightenment, while the Maha Mrityunjaya Mantra is a powerful mantra for healing and protection.

The practice of mantra chanting can also be accompanied by mudras, which are hand gestures that are believed to enhance the energy and vibrations of the mantras. Mudras can also be used to direct energy to specific parts of the body, and can be used to improve physical and mental health.

The phonetics and meaning of mantras are essential to their effectiveness. The sounds and vibrations of mantras can have a powerful effect on the mind and body, and can be used to tap into the universal energy and consciousness. Additionally, the meaning of each mantra can be used to achieve specific purposes such as healing, protection and spiritual growth. Understanding the phonetics and meaning of mantras is key to unlocking their full potential.

"Om Mani Padme Hum"
- "Hail the jewel in the lotus"

IV

The Role of Raga and Tala in Chanting

In the previous chapters, we have discussed the history, phonetics, and meaning of mantras, and how they can be used for spiritual growth, emotional balance, and physical well-being. In this chapter, we will explore the role of raga and tala in Indian chanting, and how they can enhance the practice of mantra chanting.

Raga is a melodic framework used in Indian classical music, and is often used in conjunction with mantra chanting. Raga creates a specific mood or emotion, and can be used to enhance the energy and vibrations of the mantras. Each raga is associated with a specific time of day, season, or emotion, and can be used to tap into the universal energy and consciousness.

Tala is the rhythm or beat used in Indian music, and is also often used in conjunction with mantra chanting. Tala creates a specific tempo or pace, and can be used to enhance the energy and vibrations of the mantras. Each tala is associated with a specific time of day, season, or emotion, and can be used to tap into the universal energy and consciousness.

The combination of raga and tala with mantra chanting creates a powerful and unique experience, as the music and rhythms enhance the energy and vibrations of the mantras, making the chanting more powerful and effective.

Raga and tala play an important role in Indian chanting. They create a specific mood or emotion, and can be used to enhance the energy and vibrations of the mantras. The combination of raga, tala and mantras creates a powerful and unique experience, that can be used to tap into the universal energy and consciousness. Incorporating Raga and Tala in your mantras can make it more powerful and effective.

"Om Sarvesham Svastir Bhavatu"

- "May there be well-being for all"

V

Importance of Pronunciation and Intention in Mantra Chanting

Mantra chanting is a practice that is integral to many spiritual and religious disciplines. The chanting of mantras is believed to have healing and transformative effects on body, mind, and spirit. For this reason, it is important to realize the importance of pronunciation and intention in mantra chanting.

Pronunciation refers to the accuracy with which a mantra is chanted. It is widely believed that mantras contain powerful energies, and the correct pronunciation of the syllables is thought to unlock these energies more effectively. Each syllable of a mantra has a meaning and an associated vibration, which can be unlocked with the proper pronunciation. Thus, when the mantra is chanted correctly, its greater power and potency can be activated.

Intention is the other important element in mantra chanting. Intention refers to the purpose of the chanting - the reason why the mantra is being chanted in the first place. Clear intentions are necessary in order to focus the energies that are generated by the mantra. Without intent, the energies may dissipate and the desired outcome may not be achieved. The power of a mantra is thus amplified by a consistent focus on its purpose.

The combination of accurate pronunciation and intent is a powerful tool for manifesting desired results. Mantras that are chanted with clarity and purpose often produce the greatest results. It is thus important for practitioners of mantra chanting to strive for both accuracy in pronunciation and focus in intention.

The importance of pronunciation and intention in mantra chanting should not be underestimated. It is essential for practitioners to understand the power of correct pronunciation and focused intention in order to obtain the full benefits of the practice. By ensuring accuracy and purpose, one can maximize the power of the chant and unlock its full potential.

"Om Tat Sat"
- "That is truth"

VI

The Different Types of Mantra

The Different Types of Mantra: Bija, Vedic, and Tantric Mantra.

In the previous chapters, we have discussed the history, phonetics, meaning, and the role of raga and tala in Indian chanting. In this chapter, we will explore the different types of mantras and their unique characteristics.

Bija mantras are considered to be the most basic and fundamental type of mantras. They are made up of a single syllable or word, and are believed to have a powerful effect on the mind and body. Bija mantras are often associated with specific elements, chakras, or deities, and can be used for a variety of purposes, such as healing, protection, and spiritual growth. Examples of Bija mantras include "Om", "Hrim", and "Srim".

Vedic mantras are derived from the Vedas, the oldest sacred texts of Hinduism. They are often used for specific rituals and ceremonies, and can be used for a variety of purposes, such as healing, protection, and spiritual growth. Examples of Vedic mantras include the Gayatri Mantra and the Maha Mrityunjaya Mantra.

Tantric mantras are associated with the Tantra tradition, which is a form of spiritual practice that seeks to achieve enlightenment through the use of ritual and meditation. They are often associated with specific deities or energies, and can be used for a variety of purposes, such as healing, protection, and spiritual growth. Examples of Tantric mantras include the Kali Mantra and the Tara Mantra.

There are many different types of mantras, each with their unique characteristics. Bija mantras are considered to be the most basic and fundamental, Vedic mantras are derived from the Vedas, and Tantric mantras are associated with the Tantra tradition. Understanding the different types of mantras can help you to choose the right one for your specific needs and goals. Incorporating the right mantra for your needs can make your practice more effective and powerful.

"Om Tryambakam Yajamahe"
- "We worship the three-eyed one"

VII

The History and Development of Indian Chanting

The History and Development of Indian Chanting and Mantra Traditions.

In previous chapters, we have discussed the various aspects of Indian chanting, including the phonetics, meaning, and different types of mantras. In this chapter, we will explore the history and development of Indian chanting and mantra traditions.

The origins of Indian chanting and mantra traditions can be traced back to the Vedic period, which lasted from around 1700 BCE to 600 BCE. During this time, the ancient Indians developed a rich tradition of ritual and spiritual practices, which included the use of mantras and chanting. These practices were passed down from generation to generation, and were primarily used by the priests, sages, and other spiritual leaders of the time.

During the Upanishadic period, which lasted from around 800 BCE to 200 BCE, there was a significant shift in the spiritual and philosophical beliefs of the ancient Indians. The Upanishads, which are considered to be the foundation of Indian philosophy, emphasized the idea of self-realization and the attainment of enlightenment through the use of meditation and other spiritual practices. This period saw the development of various schools of thought, including the Yoga and Vedanta, which placed a greater emphasis on the individual's spiritual journey and inner realization.

As Indian culture and religion evolved, so did the practice of Indian chanting and mantra traditions. The Bhakti movement, which began around the 7th century CE, emphasized devotion and the personal relationship between devotee and deity, rather than ritual and sacrifice. This lead to the popularization of devotional singing and mantra chanting among the general population.

During the 19th century, Indian chanting and mantra traditions were brought to the Western world by Indian spiritual leaders such as Ramakrishna, Vivekananda and Aurobindo. This lead to a renewed interest in the practice, and it began to be studied and practiced by people from different cultures and backgrounds.

Indian chanting and mantra traditions have a rich history that spans thousands of years. The practice has evolved and developed over time, adapting to the changing spiritual and philosophical beliefs of the Indian people. Today, the practice continues to be an important part of Indian culture and spirituality, and is being increasingly studied and practiced by people from different cultures and backgrounds. Understanding the history and development of Indian chanting and mantra traditions can deepen our understanding and appreciation of the practice.

"Om Namo Narayanaya"

- "Salutations to Narayana"

VIII

Power of Nada Yoga in Indian Chanting

The power of Nada Yoga in Indian mantra chanting is a potent and ancient system of spiritual practice. It has been used in the Indian subcontinent for centuries to attain inner peace, focus, and spiritual growth. Nada Yoga is said to be the path of awakening by identifying and connecting with the innate spiritual energies inside one's own body and mind. Nada Yoga is rooted in the ancient practice of chanting mantras, often in meditative states.

At the core of Nada Yoga is the belief that mantra chanting can be used to raise and intensify the frequencies of the human mind and body. Through sustained and prolonged chanting, a person is said to be able to attune their consciousness to the vibrational frequency of the mantras and access higher states of consciousness and inner wisdom. In this way, mantra chanting is seen to allow for spiritual self-realization and the attainment of inner peace and harmony.

In Nada Yoga, the use of mantra chanting is seen as a tool for calming the mind, quieting the mental chatter, and exploring our inner potential. It is seen as a way to open the doors of one's awareness to the higher spiritual vibrational levels. Mantra chanting alone is seen as a powerful practice to reduce stress and anxiety, increase mental focus, and deepen spiritual connectedness.

Furthermore, Nada Yoga is seen as a way to discover the divine energy that lies within. It is seen as a tool to access the divine energies of the universe, to access inner peace and to become liberated from the burdens and obstacles of the mundane world. Through the sustained practice of mantra chanting, practitioners are said to be able to transcend the duality of life and gain access to a higher consciousness.

In essence, Nada Yoga is a powerful, subtle and ancient practice to access higher states of spiritual awareness. It is seen as a way to connect to the potential spiritual energy of the universe and open one's doors to inner peace and wisdom. The sustained practice of mantra chanting is thought to allow practitioners to deeply connect to themselves, and explore the depths of their being. This practice has been used in India and other parts of the world for centuries and continues to serve as a source of connection to inner peace, focus and spiritual growth.

"Om Namo Bhagavate Vasudevaya"
- "Salutations to the Lord of the Universe, Vasudeva"

IX

The Role of the Guru in Mantra Practice

The Role of the Guru in Indian Chanting and Mantra Practice.

In previous chapters, we have discussed the various aspects of Indian chanting and mantra traditions, including their history and development. In this chapter, we will explore the role of the guru in Indian chanting and mantra practice.

A guru is a spiritual teacher or guide in the Indian tradition, who is considered to be an embodiment of the divine. The guru-shishya (guru-student) relationship is considered to be one of the most important aspects of Indian spirituality. The guru is responsible for transmitting knowledge, guidance, and spiritual energy to the student, and for helping the student to progress on their spiritual journey.

In the context of Indian chanting and mantra practice, the guru plays a crucial role in transmitting the knowledge, teachings, and spiritual energy associated with the mantras. The guru can provide guidance on the proper pronunciation, meaning, and use of the mantras, as well as on the best techniques for practicing them. The guru can also provide personal instruction and guidance on how to incorporate the mantras into one's daily life, and how to use them for specific purposes such as healing, protection, and spiritual growth.

The guru-shishya relationship is also considered to be an important aspect of the spiritual process. The guru is seen as a mentor and guide, who can provide support and guidance on the student's spiritual journey. The guru-shishya relationship is based on trust, respect, and devotion, and is considered to be a sacred bond between the guru and the student.

The role of the guru in Indian chanting and mantra practice is considered to be a crucial aspect of the spiritual journey. The guru is responsible for transmitting knowledge, teachings, and spiritual energy associated with the mantras. The guru-shishya relationship is considered to be an important aspect of the spiritual process, and is based on trust, respect, and devotion. Having a guru to guide you can bring a deeper understanding and practice of Indian chanting and mantra.

*"**Om Namo Bhagavate Kali**"*
- "Salutations to the Lord of the Universe, Kali"
meaning: Kali is the Hindu goddess of time, change, power, and destruction, this mantra is a way to connect with the transformative and powerful aspects of the universe.

X

Mantra in Ayurveda and Healing Traditions

Mantras have played a significant role in the ayurvedic healing tradition and Indian culture in general. A mantra is defined as a sound, syllable, word, or phrase, uttered in contemplation to direct the mind in a specific direction. It is believed that when a mantra is chanted, it creates vibrations that can help bring balance, health, and wellness to a person.

In ayurvedic healing, mantra chanting is an important part of treatment and spiritual reflection. It is believed that mantra chanting has the ability to bring positive energy into the environment, as well as bring positive energy into the patient's mind and body. According to ayurveda, each mantra chant helps to remove negative energies in the environment and to make space for healing.

Mantras are also believed to help balance the three doshas within the body, which are known as vata, pitta, and kapha. By chanting specific mantras, people can work to balance the doshas within themselves, as well as in their environment. This helps to create a holistic balance within the body and environment, allowing for better health and well-being.

Mantras can also be used to treat specific ailments. When performed correctly, mantras can help to bring more energy and clarity to physical, emotional, and mental issues. Different mantras can be used to clear emotional blocks, bring balance to an unbalanced mind, and assist with relaxation. They can also be used to increase physical strength, reduce pain, and improve overall well-being. Each mantra is chosen based on the person's individual needs.

In addition to the spiritual and medical benefits of mantra chanting, mantras can also be used to connect people to their culture. By chanting mantras, people can explore the history of their culture and gain insight into their spiritual selves. Chanting mantras in the correct manner can also serve as a form of meditation, a form of prayer, and a source of healing.

Throughout ayurvedic history, mantra chanting has been seen as an essential part of the healing process. Mantra chanting can be used to create a connection between one's body, mind, and spirit, helping to create balance and harmony. Those looking to further explore their ayurvedic healing journey should consider incorporating mantras into their treatment plan.

"Om Namo Bhagavate Saraswati"

- "Salutations to the Lord of the Universe, Saraswati" meaning: Saraswati is the Hindu goddess of knowledge, music, and the arts, this mantra is a way to connect with the creative and intellectual aspects of the universe.

XI

Relationship Between Mantra and the Chakras

Chakra is a Sanskrit word which literally means "wheel" or "circle of energy". There are seven major Chakras which are positioned along the spinal cord. They are the Root Chakra, Sacral Chakra, Solar Plexus Chakra, Heart Chakra, Throat Chakra, Third Eye Chakra and Crown Chakra. These Chakras open and close based on a person's emotional and physical health, as well as their spiritual growth.

Mantras are Sanskrit words which are pronounced repeatedly in order to create a vibration or frequency to bring the body, mind and soul into a meditative state. Many different mantras exist that when chanted can have a wide range of impacts on the body and soul. Some mantras can bring about an increase in mental clarity, while others might help to restore balance and harmony within the body's energy systems.

The relationship between Mantra and Chakras is intertwined and complementary. When chanted correctly, mantras can open and align the Chakras- thus enabling blocked energy to move freely throughout the body. The frequencies of mantras are believed to impact the electromagnetic field surrounding the body, which in turn helps to regulate the flow of energy into the Chakras. Once the Chakras are realigned and open with the vibration of the mantras, harmony and balance is restored.

Besides having a direct impact on the Chakras, chanting mantras can also benefit the body and mind in other ways. It can help to calm the mind and reduce stress, while also enhancing mental clarity of thought and increasing positivity. Physically, it can bring about relaxation and the release of endorphins within the body, which can benefit heart rate, blood pressure and digestion.

The chanting of mantras can be an extremely powerful tool in calming the body and soul and promoting alignment and balance throughout the chakras. It can also serve as a powerful medium for healing, as the frequencies created by chanting mantras can target both the physical body as well as the spiritual, mental and emotional aspects of our well-being.

Mantras and chakras have a deeply interconnected relationship that can benefit the body, mind and soul. Through the chanting of mantras, one can gain an important tool for physical, mental and spiritual healing- restoring balance and harmony to the body's energy systems.

"Om Namo Bhagavate Rudraya"

- "Salutations to the Lord of the Universe, Rudra" meaning: Rudra is a Hindu god associated with wind and storms, this mantra is a way to connect with the power and energy of nature.

XII

The Use of Mantra in Yoga, Meditation, and Daily Life

Mantra, also known as sacred utterances and syllables, has been used in yoga, meditation, and daily life for centuries and has a profound effect on the practice of these spiritual disciplines. Mantras can be used to increase concentration, focus energy, and promote physical, mental, and spiritual well-being. These ancient syllables have remained a powerful force of healing and is still sought out by spiritual seekers around the world today.

In yoga, mantras are chanted or recited to help guide the breath and focus the mind during meditative practice. When a mantra is chanted, the vibrations that come from the recitation of the sacred syllables can open, cleanse, and activate our seven chakras and help harmonize the body and mind. The vibrations also have a calming effect, allowing practitioners to achieve greater mental, emotional, and spiritual wellbeing. Mantra can also help sharpen the intellect and enhance intuition, allowing one to better tune into the world around them and receive its guidance.

Meditation is a fundamental part of many spiritual practices, and mantra can be used to aid the practice. Mantra meditation is the act of repeating a mantra on the breath to help achieve a meditative state. Repetition of the mantra allows the mind to drift away from daily distractions and thoughts, allowing for a deeper state of relaxation and clarity. Mantra can also create a powerful force of healing and can be used to reduce stress levels, improve sleep, clear the chakras, and enhance overall wellbeing.

Mantras can also be used in everyday life, as an individual or group to bring about transformation with each other. Using mantras in daily life can help cultivate a sense of focus, peace, and positivity, which can support us in making better decisions and better manage our emotions. When chanted together, mantras can create a powerful energy force that can lift the vibrations of the group and help spread a sense of community and connection.

Defenitely, mantras have a significant effect when used in yoga, meditation, and daily life. Whether alone or in a group, mantra can elevate our sense of wellbeing, promote focus and relaxation, and offer powerful healing. By tapping into the powerful vibrations of ancient syllables, we can bring balance to our minds and bodies and seek the transformation we are all striving for.

"Om Namo Bhagavate Lakshmi"
- "Salutations to the Lord of the Universe, Lakshmi" meaning: Lakshmi is the Hindu goddess of wealth, fortune, and prosperity, this mantra is a way to connect with the abundance and material well-being aspects of the universe.

XIII

Mantra in Devotional Practice and Bhakti Yoga

Mantras and chants have a significant role in devotional practice and Bhakti yoga. Mantras are words spoken with devotion and have the power to help clear away energy that blocks spirituality. The syllables of a mantra can create vibrations that can unlock certain areas of the mind, allowing the practitioner to open themselves to the Universe and make a spiritual connection. Chanting a mantra can also help a person to focus, develop patience and be in tune with their inner self.

Bhakti yoga, also known as the path of devotion, is a spiritual practice which involves chanting mantras and the devotion to a chosen deity. It is the path of surrender, of unconditional love and surrender to the Divine. By chanting mantras with awareness, an individual has the opportunity to connect with the Divine and be in harmony with nature and all that is around them.

Mantras and chanting can also assist in releasing negative energy and bring peace to an individual's life. When chanted with emotion, mantras help to open up the heart and create vibrations within the body which can help to bring calmness to the mind. Repeating a meditation or phrase can bring the person into the present moment and lead them to a place of mindfulness.

The repetition of mantras can also help to cultivate self-awareness, as they remind us of the importance of staying connected to our true nature. They also help us to relax and become more accepting of our situation, allowing us to enjoy life as it is and move away from our inner struggle. Through chanting mantras or performing bhajans (devotional songs), we can strengthen our relationship with the Divine, leading to better understanding of our true purpose and how to fulfill it.

For those wishing to pursue a deeper practice of bhakti yoga and devotional practice, it is advised to learn mantras and chants from a qualified teacher in order to experience the full potential of these practices. In this way, one can gain greater understanding of the power and benefits of mantras and chants and become better equipped to live a spiritually fulfilling life.

To conclude, mantras and chanting can be powerful and transformative tools to assist us in our journey of devotion and self-discovery. As long as they are chanted with love and sincerity, they can enable us to open our heart, connect with the Divine and move towards the path of enlightenment.

ཱ

"Om Namo Bhagavate Aum"

- "Salutations to the Lord of the Universe, Aum" meaning: This mantra is a way to connect with the ultimate reality, the lord of the universe, who is symbolized by the sound Aum.

XIV

The Effect of Group Chanting

Groups chanting mantras and engaging in community practice is an increasingly popular practice. This practice has a powerful effect, both on the individual and on the collective. On an individual level, it can lead to increased peace, calm, and clarity. On a collective level, it can foster harmony, connection, and unity.

For individuals, the practice of chanting mantras in a group strengthens their connection to the sacred, which is often associated with the experience of inner peace. When a mantra is chanted in a group, it can create a vibration of energy that can be felt in and around each person. This energy can promote healing, harmony, and connection within each individual. Chanting also encourages concentration and focus as well as relaxation of the mind and body. Being in a group and sharing the practice is a way to foster community and connection beyond the physical realm.

On a collective level, group chanting of mantras and community practice can bring people together in an unprecedented way. This can help to reduce feelings of loneliness, separation, and disconnection. Research has found that group chanting also increases feelings of unity, solidarity, and connectedness within a group. As such, it can foster a sense of social cohesion and support among those taking part. This can create a sense of harmony and shared identity that transcends differences and unites people in common values and beliefs.

All in all, group chanting of mantras and community practice can have a profound and powerful impact on the individual and the collective. Not only does it provide a sense of inner peace and connection, but it can also create a sense of solidarity and community among those taking part. In this way, it can be a powerful tool for healing and transformation.

"Om Shanti, Shanti, Shanti"

- *"Peace, Peace, Peace"*

Other Books Of The Author

1. The Moments When I Met God
2. Kashiyile Theertha Pathangal
3. GURU GYAN VANI
4. Abhiprerak Gita
5. ASSI SE JAIN GHAT TAK
6. Hopelessness of Arjuna
7. The Soul and It's True Nature
8. Sense of Action (Karma)
9. Action through Wisdom
10. Action through Wisdom
11. THEORY AND PRACTICAL OF EVERY ACTION
12. LOGICAL UNDERSTANDING OF THE SUPREME
13. THE IMPERISHABLE SUPREME
14. Yatra Nishadraj se Hanuman Ghat Tak
15. Yatra Karnatak Ghat se Raja Ghat Tak
16. Yatra Pandey Ghat se Prayagraj Ghat Tak
17. Yatra Ranjendra Prasad Ghat se Dattatreya Ghat Tak
18. YaatraSindhiya Ghat se Gwaliar Ghat Tak
19. Yatra Mangala Gauri Ghat se Hanuman Gadhi Ghat Tak
20. Yatra Gaay Ghat Se Nishad Ghat Tak
21. MAA GANGA, GHATEN EVM UTSAV
22. Ganga Arti Dev Deepavali evam Any Utsav
23. Potentials of Digitalized India
24. VEDIC CONSCIOUSNESS
25. A Brief Introduction to Vedic Science
26. Kashi ke Barah Jyotirling
27. IMPACT OF MOTIVATION
28. Let's have a Milky Way Journey
29. Color Therapy in a Nutshell

30. Rigveda in a Nutshell
31. Yajurveda in a Nutshell
32. Samveda in a Nutshell
33. Atharva Veda in a Nutshell
34. Ayushman Bhava - Ayurveda
35. Srimad Bhagavad Gita and Upanishad Connection
36. Srimad Bhagavad Gita - an attempt to summarize each chapter.
37. Facts and Impact of Nakshatra
38. Astro Gems - NAVARATNA
39. Ekadashi - A Concise Overview
40. A Concise View of Hanuman Chalisa
41. Inspirational Gita
42. Nakshatraranyam
43. Summary of 18 Mahapuranas
44. Synopsis of 18 Upa Puranas
45. Rigvediya Upanishads
46. Shukla Yajurvediya Upanishads
47. Krishna Yajurvediya Upanishads
48. Samavediya Upanishads
49. Atharvavediya Upanishads
50. The Seven Great Sages
51. From Rocket Scientist to President Dr. APJ Abdul Kalam
52. The Visionary's Voice - Quotes of Dr. APJ Abdul Kalam
53. The Wisdom of Swami Vivekananda: Insights and Inspiration from a Legendary Spiritual Teacher
54. Ayurvedic Remedies from the Garden
55. Sages and Seers
56. Rising Strong – Motivational Stories of Women
57. Beyond Flames -Mystery stories of Funeral Ghat Manikarnika
58. The Origins of Tulsi: A Look at the Mythological Roots of the Plant"

59. The Holistic Cow: A Look at the Physical, Spiritual, and Cultural Importance of Cows in India
60. Arts of Healing
61. Exploring the Divine
62. Understanding Five Elements
63. The Etymology of Ram
64. Symbols of India
65. Voice of Change (About Speeches of Great Men)
66. She Speaks (About Speeches of Great Women)
67. **Patriotism on Celluloid – Brief About Patriotic Films**
68. **The Music of Motivation: A Brief Guide to Inspirational Film Songs**
69. **Unlocking the Secrets of the Dashopanishads**
70. A Cultural Mosaic
71. Ancient Traditions, Modern Minds
72. Ecos of Ancient Wisdom
73. Beneath the Surface
74. From Temples to Ashrams
75. Sages of the Subcontinent
76. The Art of Healling (Ayurveda, Yoga & Naturopathy)
77. Indian Kitchen
78. The Festivals of India
79. The Indian Epics Retold
80. The Power of Mantras

CONTACT

DR. JAGADEESH PILLAI

PhD in Vedic Science

Four Times Guinness World Record Holder

Winner of Mahatma Gandhi Vishwa Shanti Puraskar and
Global Peace Ambassador

Gemology, Astro & Vastu Consultant - Spiritual Counselor

Consultant for designing World Record Ideas

Efficient Tarot Card Reader

9839093003

myrichindia@gmail.com

drjagadeeshpillai@facebook

drjagadeeshpillai@instagram

jagadeeshpillai@youtube

www. JAGADEESHPILLAI.com

ꙮ

|| LOKAHA SAMASTHAHA SUKHINO BHAVANTU ||

www.ingramcontent.com/pod-product-compliance
Ingram Content Group UK Ltd.
Pitfield, Milton Keynes, MK11 3LW, UK
UKHW041844200726
13854UKWH00005BA/2059

9 798889 511489